For the Teacher

This reproducible study guide to use in conjunction with a specific novel consists of lessons for guided reading. Written in chapter-by-chapter format, the guide contains a synopsis, pre-reading activities, vocabulary and comprehension exercises, as well as extension activities to be used as follow-up to the novel.

In a homogeneous classroom, whole class instruction with one title is appropriate. In a heterogeneous classroom, reading groups should be formed: each group works on a different novel on its reading level. Depending upon the length of time devoted to reading in the classroom, each novel, with its guide and accompanying lessons, may be completed in three to six weeks.

Begin using NOVEL-TIES for reading development by distributing the novel and a folder to each child. Distribute duplicated pages of the study guide for students to place in their folders. After examining the cover and glancing through the book, students can participate in several pre-reading activities. Vocabulary questions should be considered prior to reading a chapter; all other work should be done after the chapter has been read. Comprehension questions can be answered orally or in writing. The classroom teacher should determine the amount of work to be assigned, always keeping in mind that readers must be nurtured and that the ultimate goal is encouraging students' love of reading.

The benefits of using NOVEL-TIES are numerous. Students read good literature in the original, rather than in abridged or edited form. The good reading habits, formed by practice in focusing on interpretive comprehension and literary techniques, will be transferred to the books students read independently. Passive readers become active, avid readers.

Novel-Ties® are printed on recycled paper.

SYNOPSIS

A fourteen-year-old Navaho girl, Bright Morning, narrates this tale set in the 1860s. She lives in Canyon de Chelly in what is now New Mexico, tending sheep as her ancestors did.

Bright Morning's life is interrupted, however, when she and her friend Running Bird are captured by Spanish slavers and sold as household servants to the wives of white soldiers. Appearing to cooperate with her captors, Bright Morning bides her time until Nehana, a rebellious Nez Percé slave, helps her escape. The Spaniards pursue her, but Bright Morning is saved by Tall Boy, her fiancé. During their escape, Tall Boy sustains a shoulder wound that eventually disables his right arm, making him unable to hunt or be a successful warrior.

Once back at her village, Bright Morning's life resumes its normal rhythm and she is content. But this peace is broken when the Long Knives, the Navaho name for bayonet-wielding white soldiers, demand that the Navahos abandon their village and relocate near Fort Sumner. In response, the entire village escapes to the mesa from which they witness the destruction of their village and their treasured peach orchards. The white soldiers wait until the starved Navahos surrender.

The entire village is then herded together and forced to join the rest of the Navaho nation on what is now called The Long Walk. Faced with bad weather, poorly clothed, and in ill-health, many Navahos died on the forced march.

Although they were promised good land at their final destination of Bosque Redondo, the surviving Navahos are devastated when they see where they must live. This land, upon which they will be virtual prisoners, is unarrable and must be shared with their enemies, the Apaches.

Despite this adversity, Bright Morning marries Tall Boy. As a young bride expecting their first child, Bright Morning convinces her husband that they should flee from Bosque Redondo so that their child can live freely on their ancestral lands. After a difficult journey, they arrive with their new son at Canyon de Chelly, where they prefer to live at risk in a hillside cave rather than under the surveillance of the white soldiers at Bosque Redondo.

BACKGROUND INFORMATION

The Navahos are a tribe of Native Americans who inhabit the dry, rugged territory of the American Southwest. For two hundred and fifty years prior to the arrival of United States soldiers, they fought Spanish-speaking white people who lived in that region. Mexicans raided Navaho villages and camps to steal and make slaves of their young children, and the Navahos retaliated with raids against the Mexicans.

By the 1850s most of the Navahos had abandoned their nomadic lives for a settled existence, farming the land and raising livestock. In fact, many Navahos had become prosperous as herders and weavers. Manuelito, a wealthy herder who was chosen as head chief in 1855, entered into numerous treaties with the Americans.

From the start, this was an uneasy alliance: each side believed the other was encroaching upon its rightful territory and diminishing its power. In response to the wild activities of some young Navahos, soldiers from Fort Defiance raided a Navaho village, burning the hogans and killing the animals. The Americans at the Fort insulted the Navahos by allowing their horses to graze upon what had been prized Navaho pastureland; and the Navahos, who had never known fences, allowed their livestock to stray onto this pastureland. The soldiers reacted by shooting the animals that belonged to the Navahos. In a chain reaction, the Navahos raided the soldiers' herds, and the soldiers attacked bands of Navahos.

Finally, Manuelito organized a Navaho army of more than one thousand warriors and attacked Fort Defiance. The United States Army, regarding this as an act of war, pursued Manuelito and his troops for an entire year through the Chuska Mountains. Although the Americans were unable to catch Manuelito and his band, a treaty was agreed upon in January 1861 when the Navahos were eager to return to their homes and resume farming.

For a short time, the pact was observed. The Americans built Fort Wingate, and the Navahos went there to trade and participate in horse races. In one such race, when Manuelito believed his horse was sabotaged, new animosities erupted. Navahos demanding fair play and a rematch were met with American gunfire. The ensuing massacre in September 1861 marked the end of any hope for peaceful coexistence between the Americans and the Navahos.

The Civil War moved west at this time bringing with it battles between Confederate and Union forces. In 1863, when the Union soldiers drove the Confederates to Texas, General James Carleton turned his attention to the Navahos whom he regarded as savages occupying valuable land. He gave the Navahos an ultimatum: if they wanted to live in peace, they had one month to resettle in the Bosque Redondo Reservation, an arid section of land in the Pecos Mountains.

When none of the Indians surrendered, General Carleton commanded Kit Carson to prepare his troops for war against the Navahos. The Navahos entrenched themselves in the thirty-mile-long area of Canyon de Chelly bordered by the steep rock walls of the Chuska Mountains. Following a policy of burning Navaho lands, the American soldiers effectively starved out the Navahos. In March 1864, hungry and weak men, women, and children of a defeated Navaho nation began the three-hundred-mile trek that has become known as The Long Walk.

Those who survived the march arrived in a land that was unable to support them. Treated like prisoners, underfed, and ill-clothed, many Navahos died of starvation and disease. It wasn't until 1866 that General Carleton, under criticism for his Bosque Redondo policy, was relieved of his duty. Under the authority of his successor, A. B. Norton, the Navahos were allowed to return to a small, parched section of land in Canyon de Chelly.

PRE-READING ACTIVITIES

1. Read the Background Information on pages two and three of this study guide and do some additional research to learn about the Navahos in the Southwest. Find out what events preceded the Long March in 1864. Also learn about the American policy of Manifest Destiny. How was it carried out? Do you think this was a good policy?

2. Find photographs of Canyon de Chelly, which appears today much the way it did in 1860. As you view these photographs, you will be able to appreciate its beauty as well as the risk involved in establishing homes within caves in the steep walls of the canyon.

3. Look at the map on page three of this study guide and then locate its position on a map of the entire United States. As you read the book, trace the path of the Navahos when they were forced to walk from Canyon de Chelly to Bosque Redondo.

4. Historical fiction is fiction based in part on actual historical events and people and in part on the author's imagination. Discuss the following issues with your class before you read *Sing Down the Moon*:

   - Why should anyone read historical fiction and not derive history from textbooks?

   - How do authors find the factual information that serves as the underpinning of their stories?

   - What kinds of original source materials are available to authors of historical fiction?

   - How does a reader know whether information presented in a work of historical fiction is accurate?

5. Are you or is anyone you know a recent immigrant to America? Has this ever been the cause of incidents of cross-cultural misunderstanding or animosity? What do you think one culture needs to know about another in order to live together harmoniously?

6. Find photographs or actual artifacts representing Navaho handicrafts. Of particular beauty are Navaho pottery, weaving, and silver jewelry set with turquoise stones. Examples of Navaho handicrafts help you appreciate the richness of their culture and tradition as you read this book.

CHAPTERS 1, 2

Vocabulary: Draw a line from each word on the left to its definition on the right. Then use the numbered words to fill in the blanks in the sentences below.

1. mesquite
2. mesa
3. grove
4. barranca
5. goad

a. group of trees; orchard
b. drive or urge on
c. small thorny tree
d. ravine; gorge
e. high plateau with a flat top and steep, rocky sides

. . . .

1. The sheep took shelter from the rain by huddling in the aspen _____.

2. The warm spring air melted the snow and caused the water to gather under the trees and to run through the meadows and down the steep _____.

3. We stood on the high _____ observing that spring had come early in the plain below.

4. No matter how hard they _____ me to speak, I am too shy to get up on the stage.

5. We knew the sheep would prefer the first young grass to the tough and chewy _____ they had lived on through the winter.

> Read to find out about life in a Navaho village.

Questions:

1. What evidence showed that the narrator had a deep affection for the place where she lived?

2. Why didn't the girl display outward joy at the coming of spring?

3. How do you know sheep were very valuable to the girl's family?

4. Why wasn't the girl insulted when the other girls teased her?

5. What special roles did the men have in the girl's Navaho village? What were the special roles of the women?

Chapters 1, 2 (cont.)

Questions for Discussion:

1. How would you assess Navaho life as described by the narrator?

2. What qualities made Tall Boy an excellent match for the girl who was narrating the story?

Literary Device: Point of View

Point of view in literature refers to the person telling the story. Who is telling this story? What is known about the narrator? What important information about her has the author withheld? Why do you think he has done so?

_____

_____

_____

Literary Element: Setting

The setting in literature refers to the place and time in which the events of the story occur. Setting in this novel has great importance. Reread the first two pages of the novel and notice how the author evokes the senses of sight, hearing, and touch to make the setting come alive. Use the chart below to jot down the specific phrases that the author uses.

Sight	Hearing	Touch

Writing Activity:

Create a chart of sense impressions, such as the one above, for a setting that is familiar to you. Then use these phrases to write a description of this place.

CHAPTERS 3, 4

Vocabulary: Use the context to figure out the meaning of the underlined word in each of the following sentences.

1. The girl dreamed of the time when her <u>ewes</u> would give birth and she would have thirty sheep of her own.

    Your definition_____

    Dictionary definition _____

2. If the Navahos did not keep the peace, the white soldiers would <u>plunder</u> their village.

    Your definition_____

    Dictionary definition _____

3. The girl knew she would never again be so <u>foolhardy</u> as to leave her sheep untended.

    Your definition_____

    Dictionary definition _____

4. The <u>hogans</u> seemed empty and quiet on the night after the warriors left for the hunt.

    Your definition_____

    Dictionary definition _____

5. The girl's mother worried that Tall Boy was too <u>haughty</u> for his own good.

    Your definition_____

    Dictionary definition _____

6. At <u>dusk</u>, the girl and Running Deer brought their sheep back to their village from a day of grazing.

    Your definition_____

    Dictionary definition _____

Read to find out how the Spanish gained power over the Navaho.

Chapters 3, 4 (cont.)

Questions:

1. How did Tall Boy get his name?

2. What was the girl's mother suggesting about Tall Boy when she said, "I hope that he does not kill another bear. If he does he will call himself Very Tall Boy and we will have much trouble with him"?

3. What former treaty did the "Long Knives" come to enforce in the girl's village? What did they threaten to do if the treaty were broken?

4. Why did the white soldiers wield such power over the Navahos?

5. Why were the Spanish slavers able to catch the girl and Running Deer off guard?

6. What evidence showed that slaving had been a common practice of the Spaniards?

Questions for Discussion:

1. Why do you think the Navaho were so vulnerable to the Spanish?

2. Do you think the Spanish were justified in any way to claim power over the Navaho?

3. Why do you think Navaho elders taught the young not to be arrogant?

Literary Device: Personification

Personification in literature is a device in which an author grants lifelike characteristics to nonliving objects. For example:

> The sun crawled up the sky.

What is being personified?

_____

What does this tell you about the passage of time?

_____

_____

Writing Activities:

1. Imagine that you are Tall Boy setting out on a hunting and raiding expedition. In a short journal entry express your hopes and dreams for this trip.

2. Imagine that you are the girl on the night she is taken by the slavers. In a journal entry express your shattered hopes and dreams as well as your fears for the future.

CHAPTERS 5, 6

Vocabulary: Number the words in each of the following word groups so that they form a logical sequence. Then explain the logic of that sequence. For example:

	white	black	gray — light to dark	
	1	3	2	

1.	gallop	trot	canter	walk

2.	shout	whisper	bellow	talk

3.	dusk	day	night	dawn

4.	look	peek	glance	stare

> Read to find out if the girl was able to escape from the slavers.

Questions:

1. How did the Spaniards foil the girls' escape plans?
2. How long did it take for the Spaniards and the girls to reach their destination?
3. Why did the Spaniards allow the dog to remain with the girl?
4. Why did he girl sleep beside her dog in the hut of the Apache woman?
5. What warning did the girl have that life in the village would be worse than she imagined?

Questions for Discussion:

1. Why do you think the Apache woman aided the Spanish slavers? Do you think this justified her behavior?
2. Why were the two girls frightened when they saw the wolf during the second night after they were captured by the Spaniards? What did this suggest about their system of beliefs and their relationship to animals?

Writing Activities:

Imagine that you are the girl. Write a journal entry describing your feelings about your days with the Spaniards.

CHAPTERS 7 – 9

Vocabulary: Synonyms are words with similar meanings. Draw a line from each word in column A to its synonym in column B. Then use the words in column A to fill in the blanks in the sentences below.

	A		B
1.	surly	a.	temperament
2.	disposition	b.	bound
3.	omen	c.	rude
4.	bough	d.	branch
5.	tethered	e.	warn
6.	caution	f.	sign

. . . .

1. The _____ of the tree bent to the ground once the apples were ripe.

2. All the other employees kept their distance from the waiter who was known to have a terrible _____.

3. The horse was _____ to the fence so it would not run away.

4. Some people fear a black cat is a(n) _____ of bad luck.

5. The road sign was put up to _____ drivers about dangerous road conditions.

6. After several nights without sleep, the soldier became _____ to his fellow officers.

> Read to learn about the girl's life as a slave.

Questions:

1. How did the girl show defiance toward her captors?

2. Why did the woman express displeasure with the girl?

3. What differences did the girl observe between the way this woman lived and the way the Navahos lived?

4. Why was the girl pleased to hear the owl's sound at night?

5. How did the girl learn where Running Bird was living?

Chapters 7 – 9 (cont.)

6. How did the girl find out about the penalty for attempted escape?

7. In contrast to the girl, why was Rosita happy to live as a slave?

8. Why did Nehana choose the place where the *Penitentes* met to escape along with the girl and Running Bird?

Questions for Discussion:

The author has not revealed the name of the narrator, the main character in the novel. Even when Rosita asked, the girl did not reveal her real name. Why do you think the author has not revealed her name? Under what circumstances do you think the girl might reveal her name? Knowing how the Navaho select their names, what might be a suitable name for this girl?

Writing Activity:

Write about a time when you were subject to unfair treatment. Describe the situation and tell whether you showed defiance. Indicate how the situation was resolved.

CHAPTERS 10, 11

Vocabulary: Many words have more than one meaning. Read the definitions for each underlined word. Circle the letter of the definition that fits the way each word is used in the sentence.

bank
    a. rising ground bordering a body of water
    b. cover a fire with ashes or earth
    c. money-lending institution

1. The girl and Running Bird walked along the <u>bank</u> until they reached a place where they could cross.

bit
    a. single unit of information
    b. mouthpiece of a bridle
    c. past tense of "to bite"

2. The horse came to a halt when the reins pulled back on the <u>bit</u> in its mouth.

crop
    a. harvest
    b. short riding whip
    c. cut the top off

3. We watched the sheep as they <u>cropped</u> the tender young shoots of grass in the field.

current
    a. flow, as of a river
    b. present
    c. flow of electricity

dashed
    a. struck or smashed violently
    b. ruined or frustrated hopes
    c. rushed

4. The strong <u>current</u> <u>dashed</u> our canoe violently against the rocks.

draw
    a. pull; transport
    b. dry bed of a stream
    c. sketch

5. We stayed there in the <u>draw</u> until the snow stopped.

> Read to find out how Tall Boy came to the girls' aid.

Chapters 10, 11 (cont.)

Questions:

1. Why wouldn't Nehana strike a bargain with the woodcutter?

2. Why were the Spaniards able to overtake the girls?

3. How did Tall Boy's daring and bravery help the girls in their escape?

4. What was the effect of Tall Boy's war cry?

5. How did the girl care for Tall Boy after he was wounded?

Questions for Discussion:

What do you think will happen to Tall Boy as a result of his wound? What do you think will happen to his relationship with the girl?

Writing Activity:

Imagine you are the girl and write a journal entry describing your thoughts and feelings on the day Tall Boy was wounded.

CHAPTERS 12, 13

Vocabulary: Use the context to determine the best synonym for the underlined word in each of the following sentences. Circle the letter of the word you choose.

1. They placed the boy's wounded body on the <u>litter</u> and carried him back to the village.

   a. mattress   b. wagon   c. stretcher   d. operating table

2. The young man appeared <u>gaunt</u> after spending two years in a prisoner-of-war camp.

   a. plump   b. thin   c. attractive   d. deformed

3. The stem of the flower became <u>limp</u> shortly after it was removed from the water.

   a. flabby   b. rigid   c. discolored   d. dry

4. The men of the tribe <u>taunted</u> the boy because he did not want to hunt or go to battle.

   a. followed   b. relieved   c. uprooted   d. teased

5. The elders of the tribe believed that the <u>spirits</u> of their dead ancestors roamed the village.

   a. ghosts   b. dreams   c. adults   d. illusions

> Read to find out how Tall Boy's life changed when he returned home.

Questions:

1. How did the girl's parents and friends react when she returned to the village?

2. How did the medicine man treat Tall Boy for his wound?

3. Why do you think the girl's mother wouldn't let her daughter put aside the planting for one day and cook deer meat for Tall Boy?

4. Why did the Navaho perform the ceremony of Kin-nadl-dah?

5. What qualities of womanhood were displayed and tested during the four-day womanhood ceremony?

6. Why did Tall Boy criticize the girl for running fast and tell her that he had not planned on rescuing her?

Chapters 12, 13 (cont.)

Questions for Discussion:

1. How do you think Tall Boy's life will be changed as a result of the wound he sustained during the girl's rescue?

2. What ceremonies in your culture celebrate a young person's passage into maturity?

3. Why do you think the Navaho treated Tall Boy so harshly?

Literary Device: Simile

A simile is a comparison of two unlike objects using the words "like" or "as." For example:

> The trees that grew there shone as if they were on fire.

What is being compared?

_____

What is the effect of this comparison?

_____

_____

Writing Activity:

Pretend you are Tall Boy. You are unable to talk about your feelings to anyone. Write a journal entry describing your feelings about your injury, your feelings toward the girl, and your hopes and fears for your future.

CHAPTERS 14 – 16

Vocabulary: Analogies are equations in which the first pair of words has the same relationship as the second pair of words. For example: YOUNG is to OLD as DAY is to NIGHT. Both pairs of words are opposites. Choose the best word from the choices given to complete each of the analogies below. Circle the letter of the word you choose.

1. SMILE is to SCOWL as _____ is to UNSAFE.

   a. dangerous   b. frown   c. secure   d. cautious

2. HARVEST is to REAP as CRACK is to _____.

   a. sow   b. crevice   c. mountain   d. plant

3. STATE is to NATION as FAMILY is to _____.

   a. cousin   b. group   c. clan   d. county

4. SEARCH is to _____ as MENACE is to THREAT.

   a. scan   b. pray   c. magnify   d. discover

> Read to find out why the Navahos left their village.

Questions:

1. How did the girl's tribe respond to the Long Knives' orders?

2. How did the Navahos mistake the intentions of the Long Knives? What did this reveal about the Navaho character?

3. How did the soldiers make certain that the Navahos could no longer live in their village?

4. Why did the girl's father decide that the tribe had to leave the mountain?

5. What was the result of Tall Boy's poorly aimed lance?

Questions for Discussion:

1. Why do you think Tall Boy left the young warriors and joined the tribe in the hillside?

2. Why do you think the Navahos did not weep when they saw their ruined fields?

Chapters 14 – 16 (cont.)

Author's Style:

Reread the portion of Chapter Fifteen that described the destruction of the peach orchards. What phrases does the author use to make the deed seem like a heartless massacre?

_____

_____

_____

_____

Writing Activity:

Of all the terrible things that happened to the Navahos, the girl suffered most because of the destruction of the peach orchards. Why did this represent the most serious loss to her? Write a short essay telling about the one thing you know that would represent the most serious loss to you. Indicate why this would be such a great loss in your life.

CHAPTERS 17 – 19

Vocabulary: Many words have multiple meanings. Circle the letter of the definition that best fits the way each word is used in the sentence.

bitter
    a. having a harsh taste
    b. hard to bear
    c. sarcastic

1. The sky was gray and the air smelled of <u>bitter</u> winds.

slipped
    a. blundered
    b. moved smoothly
    c. lost one's footing

2. Tall Boy <u>slipped</u> into our camp and lay down by the fire.

league
    a. group of teams
    b. alliance
    c. about 3 miles

3. We traveled wearily and made scarcely a <u>league</u> during the whole morning.

brush
    a. thick growth of shrubs
    b. sweep
    c. implement consisting of bristles attached to a handle

4. The land was covered with gray <u>brush</u>.

> Read to find out about life for the Navahos at Bosque Redondo.

Questions:

1. What hardships did the Navahos endure on the trail to Fort Sumner?

2. How did the girl's mother and father each view their sad situation?

3. What caused the girl's mother to cry for the first time since their journey began?

4. What evidence revealed that the white men had not prepared Bosque Redondo for the settlement of the Navahos?

Chapters 17 – 19 (cont.)

5. Why was it unwise to place the Navahos and the Apaches together at Bosque Redondo?

6. How did the new way of life at Bosque Redondo kill the spirit of both the men and the women of the Navaho tribe?

Literary Devices:

I. *Foreshadowing*—Foreshadowing refers to those clues an author provides to suggest what is about to happen in the novel. How did Tall Boy's injury foreshadow the fall of the Navaho nation?

_____

_____

II. *Symbolism*—A symbol is an object, a person, or an event that represents an idea or a set of ideas. What did the arrival of Meadow Flower symbolize to the girl? What did her death symbolize?

_____

_____

III. *Simile*—What is being compared in the following simile:

> They [Navahos] came from all directions . . . It was like a storm when water trickles from everywhere and flows into the river . . .

_____

What is the effect of this comparison?

_____

_____

Writing Activity:

There is an old Native American saying, "Do not judge another until you have walked for a day in his moccasins." Think about the conditions of the Navahos and "walk in their moccasins." Write a letter to the President of the United States from the point of view of the Navahos.

CHAPTERS 20 – 23

Vocabulary: Draw a line from each word on the left to its definition on the right. Then use the numbered words to fill in the blanks in the sentences below.

1. ramparts
2. crimson
3. gnarled
4. corridor
5. scold
6. forsaken
7. spindly

a. narrow passageway
b. abandoned
c. fortifications
d. dark red
e. find fault; reprove
f. long, thin, and frail
g. twisted

. . . .

1. The newborn colt wobbled on its _____ legs.

2. The family rescued the baby that had been _____ on its doorstep.

3. A _____ sky at sunset usually predicts a beautiful morning.

4. The soldiers had to retreat when their weapons could not penetrate the _____ surrounding the fort.

5. We walked along the _____ glancing inside the rooms along each wall.

6. The young mother did not want to _____ her child in public even though he was misbehaving.

7. We treasured the old oak tree on our property even though it was _____ and bent.

> Read to find out whether Tall Boy and his wife made a life for themselves outside Bosque Redondo.

Questions:

1. What evidence showed that the Navahos retained some of their old customs at Bosque Redondo?

2. Why was Tall Boy more acceptable as a husband at Bosque Redondo than he had been at Canyon de Chelly?

Chapters 20 – 23 (cont.)

3. What promise did the girl make to herself during the hard winter at Bosque Redondo?

4. What evidence showed that the Navahos were losing their native treasures?

5. How did Tall Boy's indecision about leaving Bosque Redondo point up the difference in attitude between the Navaho men and women?

6. Why was Bright Morning more anxious to return to Canyon de Chelly than was her husband?

7. Why was life better for Tall Boy and his wife in Elk-Running Valley than in the protected environment of Bosque Redondo?

8. Why would the cave dug into the side of the canyon provide Tall Boy and Bright Morning with a good home?

Questions for Discussion:

1. Do you think the Long Knives were justified in punishing Tall Boy?

2. Do you think the author intended this book to have a happy or a sad ending?

Literary Device: Symbolism

What did it symbolize when Bright Morning broke her son's toy spear?

_____

_____

Writing Activities:

1. Write about a real or imagined time when you had to move to a new place. Compare your new home to the old and tell why it is better or worse than the place you once lived.

2. Imagine you are Bright Morning. Think about the things you want your son to know—the story of your early life, your capture, your escape, The Long Walk, and your new home. Write a letter to him telling of these things and your dreams for his future.

CLOZE ACTIVITY

The following passage has been taken from the beginning of Chapter Fourteen. Read the entire passage, and then fill in each blank with a word that makes sense in context. Afterwards you may compare your language with that of the author.

The pinto beans pushed up through the earth and the peaches began to swell.

Wool from the shearing was stored _____ [1] for winter weaving. My father

and _____ [2] went into the mountains and brought _____ [3] deer

meat which we cut into _____ [4] and dried. It was a good _____ [5]

and a good autumn.

Then early _____ [6] winter morning three Long Knives came.

They _____ [7] from the white man's fort and _____ [8] brought

a message from their chief. _____ [9] all of our people were gathered

_____ [10] the meadow one of the soldiers _____ [11] the

message, using Navaho words. He _____ [12] fast and did not speak clearly,

_____ [13] this is what I remember.

People _____ [14] the Navaho Tribe are commanded

to _____ [15] their goods and leave Canyon de

_____ [16].

The Long Knife read more from _____ [17] paper which I do not

remember. _____ [18] he fastened the paper to a _____ [19] where

all in the village could see _____ [20] and the three soldiers rode away.

There _____ [21] silence after the soldiers left. Everyone was

_____ [22] stunned to speak or move. We had been threatened before by the

Long Knives, but we lived at peace in our canyon, so why should they wish to harm us?

POST-READING ACTIVITIES

1. Each major character in *Sing Down the Moon* represented a whole group of people and how the events of history affected that group. Match each character on the left with the group he or she represented on the right.

   1. Bright Morning

   2. Tall Boy

   3. Bright Morning's mother

   4. Bright Morning's father

   5. Little Rainbow

   a. Navaho men who became lazy and lived in the past

   b. rebellious Navaho warriors who were defeated by the white soldiers despite their courage

   c. young Navaho women who tried to save their dying children on The Long Walk

   d. Navahos who considered themselves survivors willing to risk danger in order to retain some parts of their traditional way of life

   e. Navahos who believed their way of life was totally doomed and had no hope for the future

2. Although Scott O'Dell never directly blamed the white soldiers, there is no doubt that this book is highly critical of their actions toward the Navahos. Review those events that revealed the soldiers as insensitive, inhumane, and brutal. Discuss the ways in which the soldiers went beyond their direct orders to create misery among the Navahos.

3. According to O'Dell's portrayal of the Navahos, how did they face adversity? Why do you think this attitude was an advantage prior to the arrival of white people, but contributed to the collapse of Navaho culture after the arrival of white people?

4. Read any social studies textbook with a copyright date before 1950 in which there was no information about The Long Walk of the Navahos. Then compare it to a contemporary text in which there is most likely a brief reference to this tragedy in American history. What is the effect of selection in historical texts and why has the story of Native Americans been neglected in our nations' textbooks?

5. Conduct some historical research of your own about the Navaho way of life and The Long Walk. If possible, read original documents to see a broad range of opinion concerning the events fictionalized in this book.

6. Although this book deals primarily with the Navaho nation, the tragedy recounted here was similarly experienced by other Native Americans across this country. Research the life style and history of other important tribes in America. Develop a map showing the location of each tribe.

SUGGESTIONS FOR FURTHER READING

Alter, Robert. *Time of the Tomahawk*. Putnam.

Beal, Merrill D. *I Will Fight No More Forever*. University of Washington Press.

* Borland, Hal. *When the Legends Die*. Random House.

Brown, Dee. *Wounded Knee: An Indian History of the American West*. Random House.

* Byars, Betsy. *Trouble River*. Penguin.

* Craven, Margaret. *I Heard the Owl Call My Name*. Random House.

Eckert, Allan. *Blue Jacket*. Little, Brown.

Fall, Thomas. *The Ordeal of Running Standing*. McCall.

Frank, Hebert. *Soul Catcher*. Putnam.

Fry, Allan. *Came a Long Journey*. Random House.

Hale, Janet C. *Owl's Song*. HarperCollins.

Knudson, R. *Fox Running*. HarperCollins.

Kroeber, Theodora. *Ishi, Last of his Tribe*. Random House.

* Miles, Miska. *Annie and the Old One*. Little, Brown.

Peck, Robert Newton. *Fawn*. Little, Brown.

* Richter, Conrad. *Light in the Forest*. Random House.

Storm, H. *Seven Arrows*. HarperCollins.

* Speare, Elizabeth G. *Sign of the Beaver*. Random House.

Some Other Books by Scott O'Dell

Alexandria. Random House.

The Amethyst Ring. Houghton Mifflin.

* *The Black Pearl*. Random House.

Black Star, Bright Dawn. Random House.

The Castle in the Sea. Random House.

* *Island of the Blue Dolphins*. Random House.

* *Sarah Bishop*. Scholastic.

* *Streams to the River, River to the Sea*. Random House.

Zia. Random House.

NOVEL-TIES Study Guides are available for these titles.

ANSWER KEY

Chapters 1, 2
Vocabulary: 1. c 2. e 3. a 4. d 5. b; 1. grove 2. baranca 3. mesa 4. goad 5. mesquite
Questions: 1. It was clear that the narrator had a deep affection for the place where she lived because she extolled the beauty of the river and the orchards. 2. The girl did not display joy at the coming of spring because she believed the gods punished those who showed joy. 3. It became clear that sheep were valuable because the girl had been instructed never to leave them alone; the mother and daughter braved a storm to rescue them; the girl was not allowed to watch the sheep again after she left them alone; and sheep were a girl's dowry. 4. The girl wasn't insulted because her people were accustomed to tease and joke with one another. 5. The men were warriors and hunters; the women mostly owned and tended the sheep.

Chapters 3, 4
Vocabulary: 1. ewes–female sheep 2. plunder–lay waste and rob 3. foolhardy–reckless; foolish 4. hogans–Navaho homes 5. haughty–disdainfully proud 6. dusk–sundown
Questions: 1. Tall Boy took his name on the day he killed the brown bear. 2. The girl's mother was afraid that Tall Boy would become too arrogant. 3. In exchange for keeping the peace and not conducting any raids, the "Long Knives," or the white soldiers, vowed to leave the Navahos alone. If raids resumed, the soldiers vowed to burn their village and crops. 4. The power of the white soldiers was based upon their rifles and bayonets. 5. Running Deer and the girl were caught off guard because they were intent upon tending their sheep and enjoying the beauty of the land. They did not notice the two riderless horses the men brought along to use for their captives. 6. The practice of slaving was such common knowledge the girl knew that they were going to be sold as servants in another town.

Chapters 5, 6
Vocabulary: 1. walk, trot, canter, gallop; slow to fast 2. whisper, talk, shout, bellow; soft to loud 3. dawn, day, dusk, night; light to dark 4. peek, glance, look, stare; short to long [Each of the sequences is also correct in reverse.]
Questions: 1. The Spaniards tied up the girls before going to sleep, and they rode at night when escape wasn't possible. 2. It took the Spaniards and the girls four suns or four days to reach their destination. 3. The Spaniards allowed the dog to stay with the girl because they knew that happy servants did better work and brought higher prices. 4. The girl slept beside the dog because she believed the woman might kill the dog and use it for food. 5. The furtive glance that the girl received from another servant girl who was sweeping alerted the narrator to the perils she faced in the village.

Chapters 7 – 9
Vocabulary: 1. c 2. a 3. f 4. d 5. b 6. e; 1. bough 2. disposition 3. tethered 4. omen 5. caution 6. surly
Questions: 1. The girl showed her defiance by refusing to eat, smile, or talk. 2. The woman expressed displeasure because she wanted a girl with a sweet disposition who could greet guests and wait on tables. She resented the girl's surly disposition, her cracked tooth, and pigeon-toed walk. Also, she wanted to bargain with the Spaniard for a lower price for the servant. 3. The living quarters in this home were much larger than the hogan. There were separate rooms unlike the common room in the hogan. Navahos ate with their hands out of a common pot and slept on the floor, rather than in a bed. 4. The girl was pleased to hear the owl because it was a familiar sound of home and seemed like a good omen. 5. The girl found out where Running Bird was living when Nehana, the Nez Percé girl, told her secretly in the market one day. 6. Rosita warned the girl that Nehana had tried to escape and was beaten with a leather whip. 7. Rosita was happy to live as a slave because she came from a poor tribe and liked the food, clothing, and little bit of money she obtained from her mistress. Also, she was taken away from her own tribe at the age of nine, whereas the girl was fifteen when she was kidnapped. 8. Once the *Penitentes* reached a frenzy, the girls could take their horses and escape in darkness.

Chapters 10, 11
Vocabulary: 1. a 2. b 3. c 4. a, a 5. b
Questions: 1. Nehana wouldn't strike a bargain with the woodcutter because she could not ride without a bit and bridle, and she felt she could get away from him safely. 2. The Spaniards were able to overtake the girls because they were not skilled riders and probably did not know the terrain. 3. Tall Boy faced the Spaniards and killed one of the pursuers; thus, enabling the girls to escape. 4. The sound of the war cry scared the Spaniard's horse, threw the Spaniard off guard, and reinforced Tall Boy's own bravery, allowing him to kill the Spaniard with his sword. 5. After he was wounded, the girl sat with Tall Boy, brought him water, made a carrying sled, and rode on ahead for the medicine man.

Chapters 12, 13

Vocabulary: 1. c   2. b   3. a   4. d   5. a

Questions: 1. Because they thought they were seeing the ghost of the girl, the parents and friends of the girl just stared for a while before greeting her. 2. To cure Tall Boy, the medicine man cleaned his wound with water and the juice of herbs, and then he touched his body with blue stones. 3. The girl's mother did not want to encourage the relationship between Tall Boy and her daughter since he would never be a man in his own eyes and in the eyes of his tribe. Practicality outweighed emotional considerations. 4. The Navaho performed the ceremony of Kin-nadl-dah to celebrate a girl's passage to womanhood. It announced that a girl had reached maturity and was ready to marry. During the four days of the ceremony, there were tests of her womanly strength as well as general feasting. 5. The qualities of beauty, industriousness, and obedience were tested during the four-day womanhood ceremony. 6. Tall Boy criticized the girl for running fast because he was torn between pride and self-pity. He didn't want the girl to feel sorry for him.

Chapters 14 – 16

Vocabulary: 1. c   2. b   3. c   4. a

Questions: 1. Knowing they could not resist so many soldiers, the girl's tribe decided to flee into the mountains and return to the canyon after the soldiers left. 2. Since the Navahos thought that the Long Knives would only stay in the canyon for a short time and then leave them alone, they only took provisions for five days. This revealed the Navaho qualities of trust and innocence. 3. The soldiers made certain the tribe would not return by burning the hogans, the crops, and the orchards. 4. The girl's father decided the tribe had to leave because their food had run out, water was hard to obtain, Old Bear died, and many people were weak and sick. 5. Tall Boy's poorly aimed lance revealed the Navahos' presence, and the entire clan had to return to the canyon to join the march into captivity. Tall Boy was humiliated.

Chapters 17 – 19

Vocabulary: 1. b   2. b   3. c   4. a

Questions: 1. The Navahos endured severe cold and snow on the trail to Fort Sumner. The scarcity of food caused weakness and sickness, and the Navahos were cruelly prodded along by the soldiers. 2. The father expressed optimism saying that things would be better and that they had a future in their new settlement. The mother, on the other hand, saw only death and an end to their culture in the future. 3. The sight of the barren land at Bosque Redondo, confirming their worst suspicions, caused the girl's mother to cry for the first time since their journey began. 4. It became clear that the white men had not prepared Bosque Redondo for the Navahos because they had to use driftwood to build lean-tos, and the only food given to them was wheat flour which made them sick. 5. It was unwise to place the Navahos and the Apaches on the same reservation because these two tribes had never gotten along; there were not enough resources for both tribes on this land; and the Apaches had a more aggressive character than the Navahos. 6. The men were disheartened because they could not hunt and had to perform farming tasks, which had been women's work. This left them emasculated and idle much of the time. The women had no sheep to tend or corn to grind. They felt useless since their primary tasks had been taken away from them.

Chapters 20 – 23

Vocabulary: 1. c   2. d   3. g   4. a   5. e   6. b   7. f;   1. spindly   2. forsaken   3. crimson   4. ramparts   5. corridor   6. scold   7. gnarled

Questions: 1. It was clear that the Navahos retained some of their old customs because there were marriage negotiations for the girl and Tall Boy, as well as a traditional wedding ceremony. 2. Tall Boy was a more acceptable husband at Bosque Redondo because hunting was no longer a part of the Navaho life and Tall Boy was willing to help with domestic chores. 3. The girl vowed to return to Canyon de Chelly. Her baby was due in five months and she was determined that it would not be born at Bosque Redondo. 4. It was clear that the Navahos were losing their native treasures when the girl's father traded a silver and turquoise belt for a horse, and she later trader her jewelry for blankets. 5. The men had given up and had no plans for the future. The women were stronger, more realistic, and were willing to work for a new life. 6. Bright Morning missed her own land and the sheep to tend. She dreamed that some of the sheep were still alive. Tall boy never had sheep, and he feared living in a place that would be watched by the soldiers. 7. In Elk-Running Valley, Tall Boy and Bright Morning could hunt and live in their traditional way, as opposed to life at Bosque Redondo which led to indolence and frustration. 8. The cave could not be reached by white soldiers, it was near their ancestral home, there were wild plums available, and some of the sheep that had gone wild could be reclaimed.